SIGNALS FROM THE SAFETY COFFIN

John Engels

University of Pittsburgh Press

Feffer and Simons, Inc., London
Manufactured in the United States of America

F 1 *

Library of Congress Cataloging in Publication Data

Engels, John.
Signals from the safety coffin.

(Pitt poetry series)
Poems.
I. Title.
PS3555.N42S5   811'.5'4   74–17525
ISBN 0–8229–3291–1
ISBN 0–8229–5255–6 pbk.

Acknowledgment is made to the following publications in which some of these poems first appeared: *The Atlantic Salmon Journal, Carleton Miscellany, Chicago Review, Hudson Review, Jam To-Day, Messages, Prairie Schooner, Quarterly Review of Literature,* and *The Yale Review.*

"From the Source," "Sestina: My Dead in the First Snow," "*Terribilis est locus iste*," and "The Bed" were first published in *Antaeus.*

Parts 1 and 2 of "An Angler's Vade Mecum" originally appeared in *The New York Times.* © 1970/1971 by The New York Times Company. Reprinted by permission.

"Spring Prophecy" first appeared in the *Sewanee Review* 83 (Winter 1975). Copyright by the University of the South. Reprinted by permission of the editor.

Behold, in the lout's eye,
Love.

—Roethke

Contents

I

Signals from the Safety Coffin

When in Wisconsin

When in Wisconsin where I once had time
the flyway swans came whistling
to the rotten Green Bay ice and stayed,
not feeding, four days, maybe five, I shouted

and threw stones to see them fly.
Blue herons followed, or came first.
I shot a bittern's wing off with my gun.
For that my wife could cry.

My neighbor's wife mistook the spawnditch frogs
for wood ducks nesting the white pines
up on Bean Hill: I straightway
set her right. Each April on the first

rain night I lantern-hunt for salamanders
where they hide toewalking the bottom
mucks and muds. I shudder
at the scored skin of their sides, the deep

flesh tucks. In hand they dry. I walk
in frogspawn jellies on my lawns. One time I hoped
the great white birds might brake
for the frog ditch and alight,

but all the addled past falls in on itself,
splash rings close inward on the rising stone,
my gun sucks fire, the bone becomes
whole bone, light narrows back

on filament and point, the forest turns to sand,
and only season lacking source rolls round
and round till I in my turns fall forever back
clutching my stone, my gun, my light.

When in Wisconsin where I once had time
and spring beasts gorged my marrows and my tongue,
I was not blind. The red eft clambered
in my eye.

The Floods

This is celebration   the brown
yards are showing again   the floods
may be coming shortly   everyone
worries   last year
the house was surrounded and nearly carried away
ice and trout bones buried the yards until June

and I think about the river swelling
I think mud softens in the spine   the skull
buds   ribs root in the heart
the road by first spring light
is marrow brown   trees are feeding again
it's time again   it gets
awfully lonely
lonely maybe I'm
mad or
only the pretense of loving

I dream that bones float
in the stream
so fundamentally the flooding planet turns on bone
and I will turn and all my dead
and the next poem will turn on bones
and I will awaken to all
the nice pivots and neat fulcrums
and the rain will seem
like chalky pellets on the roof

I am relentless at celebration
it is spring and time for spring poems now
I favor celebration

when there is time and light lasts and I
begin to think after a winter of slant light
deflections   waverings of shadow I begin to think

of the river thrusting into the lake and the lake blown
westerly beating upstream
houseward into the narrowing channel
and in an eddy of the mainstream
under a dog otter's oak under
a cutback in a red flare of willow root
a lamb's corpse haired with elvers
some burrowing in the guts   the carrion
brain entered and leaping with spring eels

spring salmon lying starved in the current
at the edge of the fouled eddy   clots of wool
circling   sediments of blood
from the belly hole

the appetite is clearly
seasonal   I celebrate
this spring the beasts that come to gorge
themselves on plasms of
the flooded bone the
burrowed eye

Spring Prophecy

Each year near the beginning of spring
you will think you have found something again
that you once had lost and never remembered.
And because it was small and of little worth

you will remember only the losing, but for that
you will weep. It will be the shape
of a house, a tree's death, a broken
bottle, a spring wind cushioning

your face, yellow as the smell
of camphor in sheets. It will be
no more than that. And near
the beginning of spring snow will hang on in

the pockets of timothy, and water
will spread on the yellowing ice. The corn stubble
will root in orange and brown shadows,
and it will seem only an hour before a warm rain.

In the river a trout will rise under a dark
overhang of cedars, and something will be
given to you, you will have a vision: one day
driving to work along the River Road

you will see the convergence of the road
to be no farther than the end of a hallway,
a fog boiling in the cut, no farther
than the far wall of your room, brown

as the smell of timbers. There will be
a death somewhere, the cellar of an old house
will fill up with smashed bottles, there
will be a snarl of rotting dresses, papers

spilling down a muddy stairwell. This death
will be behind you, in another town, but you
will be reminded by friends. You will think
you have found something again, but in a day's time

you will have forgotten.

Fall Inventory

The car shudders with Mozart
in the driveway
flutes and harpsichords

the timothy lawn is in fall growth
too wet and nearly too long
to cut   one hundred years ago

some lurching itinerant bay-window builder
hit it big in this dark-parlored village
and my house was his uneasy first

and practice job   he was
soon followed by an itinerant front-porch
builder whom no one hired

after my front porch had eaten up
two twelve-light windows
and a Christian door

the car doors
stand open like yellow wings
and the car sings in the driveway

flutes and harpsichords
a confident builder of off-center dormers
came along after the front-porch man

and possessed by some notion
of symmetry died
of half the job

an inventory of trees
shows one burly abdominous maple
single-limbed and sparely green

and one great yellow poplar
hemmed in by utility wires   dead
from roadsalt or detergents

the bedroom-window white pine went
in a spring two years ago clearly
detergented to death

while this summer the young maple
in the front yard began dying redly
just for the hell of it

and two rank poplars stick it out
bristling with widow-makers
back to the house   the cellar hole

springs up in fungoid cupolas
and when I am dead an itinerant turret maker
will find some way of bricking in

the dormer porch bay window with
offplumb towers   canted battlements
and crooked embrasures   living

I cannot get the kids to close
house or car doors when they run outside
to tangle on the lawn

the lawnmower clogs and stalls
one knows where centers ought to be
when porch sills rot away and floors

have dropped four inches and the car
stands open ludicrous with
song   O Christ but everything

is added on   I sulk
in my bay window   past
the bullseye lights

from high up poplar
deadfalls whistle
down

Halloween

Lying in wait for the egg throwers,
the neighborhood hoodlums, hidden
in the yard's dark, in the thickets
of the driveway willow, my shadow

from house light long
over the grass, they, invisible
in the cow field across the street,
likewise hide and wait and cry out

against my house and do not know
I listen, or hope I do. And I
listen, the narrow dead yellow of the leaves
whipping my face.

I am crept in upon. The old house
shakes with wind. The dark sky
darkens more. I am pasted all over
with yellow leaves

and the tendrils of my bones lengthen,
twine out and fix into the grass.
I think I can wait forever, and then
raucous with joy they move, they move

against me, and the egg at the end
of its high invisible arc
shatters in yellow plasms
on the window glass.   They run

away, they have done what they came for.
And I have waited for nothing again, another
year, my boundaries broken, my house smeared.
Come back, you own this house, I cannot

enter where the ignorant sleepers and safe
dreamers in the warm rooms are dark
as cow fields; they call back and forth
between themselves in dreams. I am

not blind or deaf: *You out there,*
you move and imagine you are invisible,
no different from the shadows of hollows,
grass and hill: I call you in, you

who hunt me, who have
no bed or garden of your own. For you
I will wait forever,
shaking with wind and rage.

13

The Mailbox

The mailbox is down again,
knocked in the ditch by the snowplow.
It is the fourth time this month.
Isham, the driver, doesn't care.

He watches me when we pass.
He turns to stare out the back
window of his cab. And when
I am home again and think to look, there

across the road the mailbox
is down, half-buried in snow.
I've never spoken to Isham.
I wrote in behalf of my mailbox,

but only once, and he never
answered. It was then
he began to watch. Weekly I prop
the mailbox up; I chop an inadequate

hole in the frozen dirt, and wedge
the post with broken sticks. It stands
wavering, lopsided, the door
hanging down like a broken jaw.

The flag is jammed, and if
I'm not careful, I think there's mail,
maybe a letter from Isham: "Dear Sir:
I got nothing against your goddam mailbox,

I'll be more watchful in the future. Sincerely,
Henry Isham." Not yet, though, nothing
but *Natural History*, bills, and an occasional
sexually-oriented ad. I go to bed

fearing that Isham will pass in the night,
a great plume of sparks bursting
from his monstrous blade, and this time it may be
the house itself, and no letter will ever follow.

Hawk

I find an osprey's mummy cruciform
on a wire fence, talons fisted
on a strand, fiercely blind, the great
orbits stuck through with a whittled twig,
the beak gaping, a snake's tail protruding,

the rest the bird gorged stripped
in the gullet to a hair of ribs
and delicate convulsions of vertebrae.
Hawk and corn snake make one formal beast now,
in fierce and last formality
bone within dead bone.

I am the hunter now,
my crossboned body drying
on its sinews, my eyes also
transfixed. I read blindly
names in bones, not seeing as
my eyes see. I can read
your name and others, I

have names the spine will not accept.
I see this hunting bird is dead, that
is the first name. And blind,
that is the next.

Of Mortality and the Nature
of True Christian Stewardship

When at Night
you shall awake
to hear the rooftree
creak and shiver
and the first
cold droplets down
the cellar walls
foretell the river

*Wherein the Householder
is warned, through
ominous signs, of his
mortality . . .*

that shall a day hence
swell and rise
to quench your fires,
be, *Householder*,
not surprised:
it is God warns you
that you own
wherein you live

*that it is by God's
grace as Landlord that he
possesses the dwelling-
place wherein he resides . . .*

not board or bone,
not hinge, tooth, lock,
spoon, hair or pin.
God harries you
lest you give in
to false regard
for what He lends,
that you may know

*in manner of speaking
by reason of the Divine
Lease which, by God's
whimsy, may be
at any time
broken . . .*

and yet it is of the
nature of things & no
cause for Despair,
instead . . .

how time depends
from both the rooftree
and the bone.
And yet my friend,
do not despair:
what house God's season
shall invade
is of God's Holy

if
man acknowledge the
Divine Landlord and
His holdings, & lie
in His Holy bed in
the Grace of full
Humility & Stewardship,
though he will certainly . . .

marrows made,
while men who
pridefully repel
God's timely inroads
shall reside
amongst their properties
in Hell. Remember, then,
that all shall pass

die, there is no
help for it.

and you recline
beneath God's grass:
forswear venality and pride—
it is God's house:
you cannot hide.

A Riddle, the Answer to Which Being of Such Import It May Not Be Spoken Aloud, yet It Shall Improve the Householder to Great Benefit to Address Himself to Its Solution

I ask you this
by God's Necessity:
I have no name.
Who am I that you see?

*In which the Nameless
proclaims the Riddle
to the Householder . . .*

I alone eat
though lacking appetite.
I of all creatures drink
though lacking thirst.

*and begs indulgence while
he cites his Gluttony &
Genius in one breath . . .*

I can make fire
so that it shall not burn.
I count my fathers back until the First.
I pray to God

*he speaks of the glory of
his Patrimony &
his undoubted Piety . . .*

and that no man can doubt.
I fear the sun
as precedent to Night.
I watch the season turn

*which shall not prevent
a certain timidity when
he confront the Eternal
Cycle . . .*

by Season turned.
Whatever worm
may burrow in my bones
and famish me, I cannot do without.

*and he affirms
the necessity of
his Mortality . . .*

*God does not send me dreams:
I make my own.*

*yet concludes in
unseemly Pride.*

Poem for My Mother

I am the only witness
that snow hurtles
and the planet frosts.

The children in bright
coats stand waiting
in the winter yard,

the yellow bus arrives,
they board and go.
And once they are gone

I hear from no one.
They leave me,
voice and color,

one by one.
The voice is first:
snow flies, and like

my children you
are the feat of my memory
as if I were dead,

breathing alone
in the sheets of my yards,
in the dusts of chalk and crayons.

I think of you.   You are
my most brilliant confusion,
sunlight interrupted by leaves,

rooms defiantly in disarray.
You walk forever in my darks;
I put no trust in language:

last night, all night,
the wind burst on my house.
In the morning

the children were waiting.
There were litters of pine twigs,
green as seaweed
on the salt snow.

The River

The air was heavy:
trout could swim,
fins tickled my legs,

the air beat
with leaves,   a trout
broke in the glide,

the graves
whistled with grass,
the pine

drowned in grass.
How still
you keep yourself.

Grass
is the fiercest voice
I know,   next

the hunger of fish,
bite of bone,
hard interlock

of roots, their soft
gathering.
Leaves.

The Pine

Locks snap.
Roots of grasses,
willows;   the pine

poisoned by winter
road salt slowly
browned and died

over one long summer,
the needles all summer
in steady fall, in gatherings

of rusty drifts
under my windows where
you slept one summer.

Owls lived in that tree:
on the calmest days
it sounded with wind,

the needles falling
sounded like wind,
the feathers of owls.

Grass roots, slow and pale,
lace into a brutal turf
that feeds on salt

and sucks the housing planet
dry.   Locks snap.
I hear the pine winds

beat on the belly
of your grave. Locks
snap in the

plasms of
my tongue.
Locks.

Year Without Summer

Stone grows
in lawns.
Bone
breaks wood.
I am neighbor
to my stones.

Lawns drown.
Rain is from North.
I knew a man
who did not
starve.

The bone resolves,
its rivers run
to ice.
Bony fish
lie starving
in the blood.   Snow
in August,   July
in ice.
You are near
with hair
like frozen grass.

Poem

God
great Eater of Stone,
your teeth are

mountains,
the spine
rots in my back,

my voice
gives way,
Hell

is when space
is available;
I want
display,
I live
in your ruined

house, in the
spines of trees,
in the ribs
of fishes, in
the falling light,
in the shadow

God in the cross
of your dead aim,
my mother dead,

a pride
of growing season
in her bones.

Moonwalk

What sticks with me is the pit
of the walker's shadow,
snatches of the white fantastic carapace
of Neil Armstrong in his

cautious dance and testing step,
the final graceless posturing
for balance in
the moon's feeble

and uninterested hold.
His shadow tracks behind him;
he has been cautioned,
and routinely vigilant looks only

sunward or at the oblique,
for in the whole blackness
of his shadow he will be able to see
nothing, will be in effect

blind either from shadow or
the coronal glare about the black
total hole of his head shape,
a simple diffusion effect,

nothing more difficult,
nothing but the illusion of sunburst
spraying outward from the crater
of the black skull, an intense

halo.   Hell, I've played
that game myself before,
I've had the dream where I
must be careful not to look back,

the skull bursting outward and the eyes
brief flares like supernovae
or bombs: how
about courage then, how about it

when the brain crumbles,
clicking as it cools,
and the teeth blackly
powder, and the tongue

drains backwards down
into the belly's open pits?
It is all in shadow:
the flickering white hero

sticks with me;
the walker climbs white
as salt from the grotesque ricketry
of his machine, the walker stares

sunward: man is
on the moon. Behind him
runs horizonally the
black cast of the freezing

shadow where the walker
must not look
back, for all time the
walker must not

look.
At sunrise
the white distance
dissolves in light before him,

the sky is the memory
of no light.
It is the first time
I have wanted to walk

here myself. I
can see the black deep
of the center drawing near,
and the man-shaped night remaining total.

Signals from the Safety Coffin

Outside in the night in the
graveyard the awakened corpse
breathes once, Count Karnicki's patented

glass ball rolling from his chest, and
—safety spring released—aboveground
alarm bells ringing, the red flag waving,

a beacon flashing. And he stares, doubtless,
up the opened breathing tube into thin moonlight,
and if I listen I hear him no matter

how feeble his cries. I know he is twisting
his ring, his fingers are slippery
with embalmer's talcum, they are swollen

as oak galls, and I will not come
to save him. *Why should I?* The sky
encloses me, I am myself a ring encircling this

bone, this bone encircling a buried blood,
and I for one unable yet to breathe
the black grains of the soil without

harm: and O how I fill my walls
sweat fat, scratch at the maggoty crotch!
I think now of Count Karnicki, moved

by the piteous cries of the Polish girl
interred alive, awakened just in time
by earth and pebbles roaring on her coffin's lid.

She cried, O she cried out! Now let
the dead from all their graves cry out
and flash their lights and ring their bells.

And this one, let him wait for someone else:
he is a gentle man, bewildered by the light,
the air, the muffled thudding of the bells.

And I am not, and I have loved this place:
why make nothing of all that? Here in the fields
of lights and bells and flags, the dead

clamoring to return, I turn to this: the raw
meat between the legs, the sunken
nipples, here, home in the chilling house,

with wind in the needles of the pine
four years dead, cut down. You have awakened
and call out for help: I answer that

whatever the dark volumes of the graves
from which the dead man whispers up his breathing tube
and flashes lights, in which the dead

tree speaks, the moon a soft explosion
in high mists, as I lie down to sleep
my silence is greater.

31

II

An Angler's Vade Mecum

An Angler's Vade Mecum

1

Remember: the simplest eddy,
course or countercourse of stream
appalls the cast fly and confounds
its aim. The hook should swim

as dun from nymph and imago
from dun, for trout lie gaunt
with waiting and grow dull
with season. Be aware

of season, know
trout color with the trees
and that the planet trembles to
a maple leaf for trout.

Therefore be cautious
how you walk the riverbanks.
The beast may starve
with hiding.

2

I have thought about it
often. I have thought
of the salmon as a difficult
fish. I have not forgotten

he lies concealed
in his run. I have fished
with the sun flooding
the orbits of my skull

so that my shadow does not
fall upon the water,
and I have raised
fierce feeding shadows

from the rocks,
and there is considerable art
in all of this; but it is best
to speak flatly

in such matters:
the salmon has eluded me.
My shadow has fallen
on the stream.

3

I cast to salmon with a rod
made of a lively cane, and nicely
fitted, the male ferrule
made to go

right home. Such tackle
promises success, or pleasure,
while with a rod soft
in the fibers

I should perhaps be made too
much aware of the beast
grown viciously shapely,
countering my hook

with the toothed hook
of the kype,
and the maniacal humpbacked
rush downstream.   I have

a *papier* model
of a salmon; I am
pleased with it, it is
most natural. As a

sportsman and angler the exact
reproduction of natural objects
appeals very much
to me.   It is

with great pleasure
that I possess this
reproduction, which looks
as if it were just out

of the water. I have not
taken salmon yet,
but perhaps in days ahead.
He is a spawning fish

and does not feed.
Strong tackle
is required.

4

I enclose   with this letter
a photograph of the salmon,
and the proud fisherman,
me.   You can see

that the salmon is better
than average for the stream. I
display him from a hawthorne
branch;   you see

the harebells and cornflowers
that bloom in his gills: my
ghillie put them there. It is

a custom. And I am there,
at left, attentive to my kill,
although I am
unsmiling, seriously staring

in the lens, because I hold
with ritual. My ghillie holds
my Hardy's celebrated
"Alnwick Greenheart,"

built suitable for mahseer,
salmon, trout and grayling,
and he fiddles with
my reel, a brand-new

"Cascapedia." The river
eddies to a shore of daisies
in the background right.
The rapids of the holding pool

are out of sight, but it was
there the crazy beast had tried
to kill a full-dressed *Beauly Snow* one/ought,
blue furred and tinseled,

orange and heron-herled,
that quartered, flittering,
across his lie, a roar of color to
exasperate the course of the minded blood

I hunt. But the biggest masterpiece
done by me was when I, not
with this but with another rod,
got a salmon in the Äaro River in

Sögndal, in
Sögn.   The weight
of this greater fish was
forty-three pounds, and I

was three hours landing it,
and you can bet it was
a strain on the rod, but
it was just as good after as

when I began.   I enclose
a second photograph of my
greater fish, and the proud fisherman,
me.   The rod in this picture,

made from well-seasoned greenheart,
was my dear friend for more
than twenty-five years.   But now
old age has claimed it.

5

When, many years ago, this rod
was built, I took it to
the Miramichi, and everyone roared
at my using such a light rod

for such strong fish, and I recall
their amazement at my handling
of two grilse when fishing for
small trout, with midge flies

on a small river.   Since then
it has killed thousands
of fish, and considering
the size of the rod this

seems adequate performance.
And with it I can reach well out
into any river, against any
downstream wind

to the farthest rising fish
with no effort, and the strongest fish
has no chance of beating
me.   I recall

one big and fresh-run salmon
who took the line under the canoe;
we could not get it
cleared, and this rod

before I knew it bent
clear round from the tip
to the center.   The tip
was a little twisted, but

within an hour was back
to shape, being cut from a
lively wood.   I killed

three or four nice fish
right after that, and finished them
quickly, time being too dear
on a sporting stream

to waste an hour on a fish.
This rod will kill a trout
in a minute to each pound of weight,
and if with this rod I cannot

handle any fish as I please,
I know it is not the fault
of the rod, which is, I say it freely,
the most perfect instrument

I have ever held
in my hands.

6

Although I have used this rod
mainly for trout on small
rivers, it has been pressed into service
for tiger fish.　　A month ago

it landed an accidental
turtle.　　I am glad to say
that in spite of this
regrettable incident

its power and accuracy have been
in no way impaired. And with this rod,
which was my father's for
thirty-five years before it was

mine, I took
a thirteen-pound salmon in the
Miramichi in eight
minutes.　　The water

was low, I walked back
onto the gravel,　　I
reeled the fish
onto the gravel, my friend

timed the play
of this fish.
A little later
when time decrees

I shall pass it on
to my son.   I have
used it for thirty years
myself, mostly

for trout in fishing
small rivers.   It is
an artist's rod, powerful
enough to kill heavy

trout, and yet
it fishes so light
I have often
loaned it to ladies.

But I think
careful copies might
be made, which will be
just as good.

III

Exorcisms

Sestina: My Dead in the First Snow

It is taking a long time.
How long it has been we cannot remember,
But the house roars like the windy spaces of a field,
And windows are trembling in some downstairs room.
Something is over now, and nothing will follow,
Except that slowly the light changes, window to window,

And trees go ashen in the wind. Snow drives on the windows
And watching it happen is what we have come to. Once there
was time
In the yearly violences, but now we have come to follow
The slide and drift of the white leaves through our rooms
Where light spins clockwise. *Remember*:
The planet spinning clockwise in its dark fields

Streaked the stars out into icy rings, the fields
Blooming at night with snow like stars. At night our windows
Closed onto the green fragrance of cut lawns, the room
Blooming with shadows, and we in time
In the seasons of our house remembered
That something was over and that nothing followed

Except we slowly change and are followed
Down the tracks of the beast-ridden fields.
O you and I are more than we remember!
Our hands melt through the frozen gardens of the windows
Into the darkness of the yard where we have taken time.
Light roars in the windy spaces of our rooms,

The windows are trembling in some downstairs room;
Something is over now and nothing will follow.
And it is time, it is taking a long time,
And the house is cold as the windy spaces of a field,
And the sun moves around the house, window to window,
And how long it has been like this we cannot remember,

But evening comes and the wind begins and we try to remember
How shadows like flowers blossomed in our rooms,
Flowers burst into blue forests on the windows,
And we walked among the trees and lions followed,
Till our hands on the cold glass burned away the fields,
And the flowers burned away, and the trees. In time

The lions too will die of the fire. Remember: we are followed
Through all our rooms; through the spaces of our fields
The sun turns on us, window to window. It is taking a long time.

O All the Dead of Ponderous Design!

I think of whales coming in from the sea like clouds or mountains
misty at gray distances, herds and pods heaving and blowing,
brows blunt to the seas, swarming in bays and harbors,
growing upon us with a monstrous delicacy, intent on the dry
beaches,
the surf booming and whitening on their flanks, above them the
whole round rib
of the sky a whiteness of gulls, until before them we move
backwards on the sand,

backwards on the sand and the whales like clouds in the round sea
swimming in the thunderous white sprays of their flukes, strand
in the green shallows, on the thin ribs of the beach snuffling for
breath,
days later the stink of greasy beach and scavenged carcasses,
the black pillows of their tongues jumping with crabs and eels,
meat furled on bright ribs.

Whales, buoyant in the sea, sleek from feeding, their spouts at
distances
like clouds or mountains, seek the beaches in the end and die,
and we know nothing of this, why with flukes and flippers driving
in damp sand
they force themselves upon the scorching flats, their eyes salt and
blind,
lungs crushed in the pliant ribs. Of their own weight
even the great sea beasts, the great dead of ponderous design.

We, sullen with longing, awaken to the stink of carrion beaches
and the green
light of water on the walls, as if in one night ourselves arisen from
the sea

to find our windows white with salt and the trees in the pastures
boiling up
like whale spouts, the ditches flashing and rolling with dolphins,
the floods upon us, the highest tides of all. We walk to the beaches
where the dead whales lie, the rain pooling in the hollows

of our shoulders, our heads set on stupid necks, modeled
like the commonest garden statues, the sea rising about our knees,
hissing in the ribs of the whale, smelling of all the world's
drowned dead,
and strand here, snuffling for breath, the sea at the far sky
rising up like clouds or mountains. O we who were the best of
blood and bone,
our glory once the praises of whales, we walk into the sea, we
breathe

the salt, pitch in light, drown, our fingers bright as minnows, we
who were the best of blood and bone befoul the waters of the
earth
forever, we clutter the buried beaches where whales graze and
fishes scream like birds.

Terribilis est locus iste

I recall
that when I held the leghorn
upside down, her head—
lemony beak gaping and crooning—
swiveled to fix in its balances,
craned calmly to see until

I lopped it away
on the chopping block
and she ran to flap in the cold-frame pit
in the seedling kohlrabi, frantic
and palsied, the cut
neck skin pursed
on the raw stem.

It is borne in upon me now
how I would stand to watch,
how sufficiently convinced
of bird fury and din
in the wholly silent yard,

the day bright and the sun fixed
among soft feathers of clouds;
but only my brain
in its dreadful balances squawked
and screamed and lay down
in the delicate tremor.

Tonight the sky drains downwards
in red trails, the sun
like an owl's eye swells,

and it is borne in upon me
how I listen,
what is heard:
the burgeoning tumor
that measures me, the orbit
blooming. Is it
the moon in silence rising
through the colors of brass,
is it the Sun or the Moon?

Come back, come back!
For in the petals of the great
fire, in the radiant gold
of its ash, I taste
my own tongue, I see
the gasping, still recognizable
skull, I am crowded
with flowers and leaves.

2

This is no age
of faith, rats at the holy
paste, and we
lying down in the ultimate tremor,

the delicate subsiding blood spray
brightening on leaves—although
it has been the simplest
dying, cleanest
of butcheries. This

is a dreadful place, it is
the House of God, the
Gate of Heaven,
and dwindles, finally,
to the bone,
so the bone teaches me,
that blessed is the man
if at all remembered.
I am appalled
by the uproars of the blood.

It is now time to consider
how far I must go
on the road cut out of ice,
how much will be given
if I do not ask,
if God is the midden
of generation,
if I, so dim of form,
am issue of God.

I regard the hen's foot
drowned in its yellow broth,
clenched like an eagle's claw,
her cleaned thighbones gleaming
in the crumbs of dumplings.

The House of the Dead

It is night and you are dreaming and you cry
out into the silence and they are all
silent around you, forever in place, and the sky's
currents are dividing around clouds like rocks
and the straight plunge of the sky is to the far

cliff edge of the world. You are fixed
in the center, you are waist-deep in dust.
They embrace you in the running darknesses, you are
daily departed from, loved, remembered, mourned
where everything is held and lost: the dead

stalled in their tracks, one foot raised in mid-stride,
the dead man met at the mailboxes, you raised up
to ride in giant exaltation to the windowsill,
mute sparrows circling your head. Now, where do you look?
You scream like a woman, but you are a man, a skulled

ghost, your voice wavering upwards into the silences,
crying out forever into the basins of your skull because
the beaked wind is on its way to riddle you
and when you awaken it will be night
and the doorways filled with no one who will speak

and for a voice the wind stirring in frozen bittersweet:
and you will rise and run to meet your own voice opening itself
but morning will open in the doorways. And you were greedy,
always,
for the spring. You recall how in your stopped autumns the
house elm
sprayed an invisible sticky sputum, and the stone pits

in the sidewalk filled with rain lakes and the ants drank there
or circled there or drowned; and the dead man was met
and the mailboxes, and you weep. O how in dreams
the dead you cannot warn affect a terrible love speech,
circling you, their tongues like frozen leaves,

brittle as frozen leaves, quick as fire, prattle and squeak
and grope in the final loving touch and stand away, then
                    stand away
and the wind is the sound a man might make with his horn at
                    his teeth
and at this hour it is night, it is nothing but night
and you are frozen in mid-stride in the first step, the sparrows

frozen and shining about your head,
a pumpkin sun fiery on green snow. And you see
as you always see the sleeper in his blind warmth
who cries out reaching out to you his voice
a leaf greening in the center of your skull.

Nothing Relents

Given o less by far to love than to my dead
it is I know the soul's defilement and joyous
beyond all touch or body lightly borne   the doors

of the house thrown open to the great lawn
alive with the shadows of birds that daylong
grow into blue mists and fogs

no less than those which cover my simple dead
with so long darkness   It is that the planet
is sodden and the gardens fail smothered by rain

that the corn yellows   the squash vines
are rank and infertile roots eaten away   that
there is a burgeoning of weeds   dandelions

bleeding like milk pigweeds hairy
mulleins   that the apple is black
with scab and the grass

in three days ankle-high and this
after the thinnest of winters   that
I scrape at green and blue molds

everywhere and my spade breaks through
into the muddy cisterns of the earth   that we
had been eating and drinking together when the flood

came suddenly to cover us   that this
is true it is true that the river broke the graveyard dikes
and burst in rapids on the headstones peeling back

the flowered turfs and earths and the dead
arisen from their graves walked upright
on the thick flood downstream to subside

into the delta and drift heaps of their bones
that we have not found them yet who walked
on water   not all of them   that some

hide from us still   nothing relents
and what if the world is a horrible fit
a knot or spasm in the sky's entrails?   **for Christ**

that the child died is beyond belief
beyond all suffering that he was named and I
that morning in the kitchen reached

a book down careful of noise but he slept beyond
all reach and sometimes that comes upon me to such rage
as now I am torn by the alarums of my own voice

to cry out into the dazzle of Thy
high noon O God such
anger festers in the tree the flood the stone such

bile and storm surge in the root and beasts
in the foul walls race the planet bursting swell'd
with ripeness fat with fatness opened to the light and I

like a blind grub twisting in light
mandibles wide in spasm the cold
talus falling back and in the chasm squirming   Once

thinking I too would die   old
unfellowed and alone   the sky a black heave
over the house   thunder

withholding itself and crows in dense flight   I
liar vessel of fury vengeance-seeker destroyer
swore then and now to lie among all name-proud

wrathful men in the dusts and stinking shades
of the house in the midst of this fall of things
stable in rage for that he was named and slept for that

but discomposed   for ghosts
still commonly walk and are seen   white things
fearful of light while this beast *here*

is nourished and has excrements
the flood falls therefore back into itself
the lawn dries and darkens with birds

it suits the dead to rest beyond all reach
what feeds therefore among us on the drowned
carcasses of moles   hides

in the mud digs
like a legged worm into the wet-haired
bellies of its beasts   inhabits us foul comb and hive

seething with famished larvae   the airs
of our dead resonant and beneath
the garden soils a

breathable air what
feeds on us our
scalps crawl

The Bed

My bedposts turned from maple
workbench boards from the margarine factory
yellow with corn oil oozed

from the unsealed dovetails
and mortises trickled and pooled
in the hot summer nights of the hot

room and all over the house new beds
grew up in rows and furrows like a school grove
a whale's rib cage yellow in the moon

on the yellow beach with the waves
growling in Virginia the ghost crabs scuttled
in pale drifts before the night was out

I'd been nibbled to my ribs

The Frog

We'll all end up   I tamed the leopard frog
up in Wisconsin when I was nine   I flayed it
I recall the ceremony of its awful crawl

tongue forking out with pain   loose-legged to
the water the raw meat stuck with sand   eyes
pushed in and the wildly gulping throat   but

then the strong dive into the patch
of pickerelweed and the pearly muscle flashed
and the crawl of the gut coil showed through

the belly wall   I crawl
in the stinking clots of yesterday's food
in the sour juices of the house I lie

awake on sandy sheets and flies bite

The Fish Dream

It came true that in Bikini when
as sudden as the mirror of a wing the light came
the wind changed and hot dust

mucked our crannies up we locked ourselves below
turned off the air so greeny stack gas
fills the passageways   topside

the flight deck blooms like Ol'
Virginny with a thousand fountains
while six times a day below in salty

shower baths we   hosed our
planted selves and held
breath   I'd lie

like a stain in my sodden bunk
and it made for dreams the umber-
scaled and yellow-spotted fish with six-

inch needle teeth creeps out on fins like weed
stems over the red-hot deck and
gorged our heads while

we from the steaming
humus of our eyes
stare on

afraid to wake

The Garden

I dream it yet by god that I'll
sprout in the rank mucus of that passage yet ploughed
and harrowed by its poison teeth and

seeded in every bloody furrow while
topside in wind and light the
garden of the flight deck washes

clean   surely nothing will survive me   nothing
I have feared   nothing
will grow there   salt

water floods the catwalks and the only
sea is green this is
true

it is all true as god's sweet gleaming garden overlay
the planet's foul belly hole and the rank
dirt burned to grow it is all true

and then as now beneath the scoured acreage
in the acid juices of the bellied
beast the seed of the first and

Eden fire burns and grows in the sour
armpit stink and wrinkle
wart grease scab knot sore

and scar we feel the first thrust
of the blazing root
I grow

I grow

The Bedroom

Clean rain on the final lilac   bats
in the chimney and the starling's nest
in white streaks down the window

dress myself   wifeside the smallest
son's a lumping in the covers   grins
like an egg to see me go   I am

leaving to write this down   notes
on a dream unaccountably remembered in which
I stare into the round mirror of a fish's mouth

and smear my face with black paint to the very
orbits of my eyes then roundly stare
back like a cat's in car light   that the

blood survives and shines back my whole life
I have known   in natural terror   in whole joy
and so it was last night dreaming

I'd come to my house and the door
opens wide upon round rooms swirling
with fire burned clean scoured out

with flames the furniture
white ashes on the floors   now
in the chilly morning room that stinks

of birds' nests his mother
sleeps and he and I burning to have me go
we stare into each other series

on series infinite and last night's fires
feed on our bones
the sun explodes

The Survivor

Unborn I rose in the memory
performed there puzzled for balance
on the spine's beam flailed and spun and

fell into the burning bed
breathed I thought
forever in dark trust   now

you all of you O wait with me
in the ravenous planet for the tombs
to crack and O if the tombs crack look

out into a yellow sand step out
with me onto ashes among leaves my own
graves are dark to me I

have myself walked on yellow sand
but on that very day I'll seize with you upon so
beloved again a yellow of sea sand that I can say

death has its fires too
and stick my tongue out to the
chalky rain

its taste

From the Source

My dears my creatures I was
back in the clamor of the thin light
coiled like a question mark

in the original stance, and stared
out from the slow blooming about the fire's
seed.   I was

frail arc of jaw and palate bone,
outburst of iris lobes, wrenched
diaphanous skull, faint

shades of bone, jerked
towards awakening but in sleep yet
sucked on my glassy hands, on

amethysts of flesh, clear pinks
and reds, white threads of vein
and sprout of the green brain down-

wards. I was spin
of ear whorl in on the roar
of the blazing oozes, basal

dusts and greening
vapors of the ocean's beds: my dears, my
creatures, come together now

in the bright salt breath. You
are the fishes of the seas that darken
in my skull's basins, O crab-

footed dancers who feed on me, tooth-
rayed scale and fin.   The spiral tusk bone breaks
the membrane of the sea, and the heart spouts.

PITT POETRY SERIES

COLOPHON

This book has been set in the Linotype cutting of Palatino types, with display in Optima. Both were designed by Hermann Zapf, and they are printed here directly from the metal on Warren's Olde Style antique wove by Heritage Printers, Inc. The book was designed by Gary Gore.